1, 2, and 3 John

Love and Hate, Light and Darkness

We love because He first loved us.

1 John 4:19

By David R. Maxwell

CONCORDIA PUBLISHING HOUSE · SAINT LOUIS

Contents

History	Date (AD)	1, 2, and 3 John
Tiberius Roman Emperor	ca. 14–37	
	33	John accepts earthly care of Jesus' mother at the foot of Jesus' cross
Paul's conversion and Baptism	36	
Caligula Roman Emperor	37–41	
Claudius Roman Emperor	41–54	
Jerusalem Council	49	
Gospel of Matthew written	50	
Nero Roman Emperor	54–69	
Gospel of Mark written	50–60	
Gospel of Luke written	55–60	
Rome burns; Nero begins four-year persecution of Christians	July 9, 64	
	66	John begins his ministry in Ephesus
Martyrdom of Peter and Paul	68	
Vespasian Roman Emperor	69–79	
Romans destroy Jerusalem	70	
Titus Roman Emperor	79–81	
Domitian Roman Emperor; demands to be worshiped as "Lord and God"	81–96	
	90	John writes his Gospel
	90–95	John writes 1, 2, and 3 John and Revelation
	100	John dies in Ephesus

An Outline of 1 John

Sometime toward the close of the first century, the apostle John wrote a Letter to Christians probably living in Asia Minor (modern-day Turkey). In this Letter, he used the simplest of language to communicate some of the most profound theology in the Scriptures. John uses simple contrasts, taken from everyday experience, like love and hate, light and darkness, to communicate deep truths about God, the devil, and humanity.

The structure of John is very difficult to discern. New Testament scholars have put forward multiple proposed outlines of John, many of which are radically different from one another. The outline proposed here is based on the observation that John writes in a circular style. He introduces a series of themes, and then he returns to the same themes over and over again. Each time he returns to a theme, he intensifies it by adding information or by making slight modifications. Because of this intensification, it might be better to classify his style as spiral rather than circular. Every revolution around the circle brings an advance.

The themes themselves are usually dualistic contrasts, such as light and darkness, love and hate, Christ and antichrists. These contrasts support John's underlying view of the world, which recognizes a cosmic battle underway between God and the devil. The battle is raging, but at the same time we know that Christ has already conquered.

I. Introduction: The Word of Life (1:1–4)

II. Cycle 1 (1:5–2:27)
    A. Light and Darkness (1:5–10)
    B. Love and Hate (2:1–17)
    C. Christ and Antichrists (2:18–27)

An Outline of 2 John

In this very short Letter, John urges his readers to walk in truth and love. John opposes people who are not keeping God's Commandments and not confessing that Jesus Christ came in the flesh. Other than that, he gives little specific information about the situation he is addressing.

I. Greeting (1–3)

II. Truth and Love (4–11)
    A. Love Means Keeping God's Commandments (4–6)
    B. Truth Means Confessing That Jesus Came in the Flesh (7–11)

III. Closing (12–13)

An Outline of 3 John

Like 2 John, 3 John is very short. However, the Letter is addressed not to a church, but to an individual named Gaius. John commends Gaius for welcoming and giving support to traveling missionaries. He then criticizes a man named Diotrephes for rejecting his authority and refusing to welcome missionaries.

I. Greeting: Walking in the Truth (1–4)

II. Commendation of Gaius's Love (5–8)

III. Criticism of Diotrephes's Lack of Love (9–12)

IV. Closing (13–15)

Introduction

Two major themes run throughout John's Epistles: truth and love. While his opponents refused to confess that Jesus is the Christ or that He came in the flesh, John insists on the truth of God's concrete actions for our salvation. His opponents felt that they had no sin and were under no obligation to follow God's Law. However, John stresses the obligation to love our brothers and sisters. John's opponents, then, had both doctrinal and moral problems.

Possibly, John wrote his Letter to counter an early form of a heresy later known as Gnosticism. Gnostics claimed to have a secret knowledge that ordinary Christians lacked. This secret knowledge informed them that the created world was evil, and that what one did with one's body was therefore unimportant. The recently publicized "Gospel of Judas," for example, was written by Gnostics.

When John presents the positive truths of Christianity in his Letters, he stresses concretely the physical reality of Christ's flesh. He also emphasizes our continuing obligation to care for the physical needs of our brothers and sisters. He does not allow the Christian faith to float away into an abstract, spiritual world.

Furthermore, John stresses the reality of the cosmic battle that is raging between God and the devil. He tells his readers that they are taking part in this battle. Also, they should ensure that they are on the side of light, love, and Christ, rather than on the side of darkness, hate, and antichrists. For John, there is no middle ground.

This lack of middle ground may be troubling to some readers. The entire First Letter is cast in terms of stark opposites. Consequently, at times John's description of a Christian sounds as if he or she can expect to achieve perfection in this life. One is either sinful like the devil or holy like God. However, John does not teach this. Already in 1 John 1, he stresses the necessity of the ongoing forgiveness of sins. It may be helpful to think of John describing us more as we will be on the day of Christ's return rather than as we are now (1 John 3:2). His goal, after all, is that we may have fellowship with God and have eternal life.

Lesson 1

The Word of Life

Unlike philosophy, the Christian faith does not derive truth from human reason. Rather, our faith is based on events that God accomplished in history. These events range from God creating the universe, to His rescue of His people from Egyptian slavery, to His return of His people from Babylonian exile. Yet the culmination of God's saving acts occurs in the life, death, and resurrection of Jesus Christ. This event is the hinge on which history turns.

But how do we have access to events that happened thousands of years before we were born? We cannot observe them for ourselves. We cannot deduce the content of these events by observing the present world around us. The only way we can have knowledge of these events is through the testimony of eyewitnesses. That is what John gives us in his First Epistle. John is an eyewitness; he saw Jesus, touched Him, and heard Him teach. As such, John is in a position to tell us the truth about Him.

Setting the Stage

John wrote his Letter to those he considered his "children" (1 John 5:21). Though it is unclear exactly where these recipients lived, it is clear that John is writing to churches. Tradition locates these churches somewhere in Asia Minor.

John's goal is to proclaim eternal life to his readers so they may have fellowship with him, with the Father, and with Jesus Christ (1 John 1:3). An important part of proclaiming eternal life is refuting false teaching regarding Christ. Much of the Letter is devoted to such refutation. Before he launches into his refutation of error, however, John establishes his credentials as an eyewitness to the word of life.

1. What is the value of eyewitness testimony? In what settings is eyewitness testimony important today?

2. Does the refutation of error make you uncomfortable? Why or why not?

We Have Touched the Word of Life

Read 1 John 1:1–3. Although the term "word of life" is not a particularly common designation in the New Testament, it forms the foundation of the message of 1 John. "Word of life" can mean the word about life, but it can also mean the word that gives life. The second sense is probably what John had foremost in his mind. Jesus is the "Word of life."

3. What examples from the Gospels can you think of where John or the other disciples saw or touched the Word of life?

4. John uses physical language to describe the Word of life, saying that he has seen, heard, and handled that Word. Imagine how Christianity would be different if the Word had not become flesh (John 1:14). How would this affect our view of

a. creation, and especially our own bodies?

b. what happened on the cross?

c. what we receive in the Lord's Supper?

d. the resurrection on the Last Day?

John's Opponents

John wrote against an early form of Gnosticism. The word *Gnosticism* comes from the Greek word for "knowledge." Its adherents claimed to have secret knowledge about God and the universe that no one else had. From 1 John we can piece together some of what John's opponents taught.

5. What do the following verses imply about the supposed "knowledge" of John's opponents?

    a. 1 John 1:8

    b. 1 John 2:4

    c. 1 John 2:22

    d. 1 John 4:2–3

It may seem strange that John's opponents claimed to have no sin, yet they did not follow the Commandments. However, this belief is a feature of Gnosticism. Gnostics believed that the physical world was not created good, but was in fact evil. Since they believed physical creation was evil, they denied that Jesus came in the flesh. They also claimed that what they did in their earthly lives did not matter since their bodies were evil.

6. Can you think of any people today who hold any of the positions of John's opponents?

Fellowship

Review 1 John 1:3. John states that the purpose of his Letter is to create fellowship between him, his reader, the Father, and Jesus Christ. Fellowship (*koinonia* [koy-nohn-EE-uh] in Greek) is a union, or communion, between Christ and believers, and also between believers.

7. How is this fellowship, or union, concretely expressed in the Divine Service? See 1 Corinthians 10:16–17, and note that the word *participation* is translating the Greek word *koinonia*, the same word John uses for "fellowship" in 1 John 1:3.

the bread & wine of communion makes one with Christ & therefore with each other

8. John says in 1 John 1:4, "We are writing these things so that our joy may be complete." How does fellowship with Christ bring joy to your life? How does fellowship with other Christians also bring joy?

a sense of belonging - not being alone strength in numbers

God's Word for Today

We are in a very different position than John. He was an eyewitness of Jesus' earthly ministry, and we are not.

9. Why is it sometimes difficult to believe the eyewitness testimony of others? What evidence does John provide to prove that his testimony is credible?

10. Although in a different way, we, too, have heard and touched the Word of Life, our Savior Jesus Christ, in the Gospel and the Sacraments. How does this both inspire and enable you to speak to others about Him as His witness?

In Closing

Encourage participants to begin the following activities:
- Make a list of the physical blessings God has granted you.

- Picture heaven in your mind's eye. In your view of heaven, does God continue to grant you physical blessings in eternity?
- Read 1 John 1:5–10 in preparation for the next session.

Close with prayer. Sing or read in unison the words of "For All the Saints" (*LSB* 677, stanzas 1, 4, 6–8). As you go through the hymn, thank God particularly for John's confession of faith "before the world" (st. 1), which we are studying; for the "blest communion" (st. 4) we have with Christ, John, and one another; and for the resurrection of the body, which is "yet more glorious" than paradise (st. 7).

For all the saints who from their labors rest,
Who Thee by faith before the world confessed,
Thy name, O Jesus, be forever blest.
　　Alleluia! Alleluia!

Oh, blest communion, fellowship divine!
We feebly struggle, they in glory shine;
Yet all are one in Thee, for all are Thine.
　　Alleluia! Alleluia!

The golden evening brightens in the west;
Soon, soon to faithful warriors cometh rest;
Sweet is the calm of paradise the blest.
　　Alleluia! Alleluia!

But, lo, there breaks a yet more glorious day:
The saints triumphant rise in bright array;
The King of Glory passes on His way.
　　Alleluia! Alleluia!

From earth's wide bounds, from ocean's farthest coast,
Through gates of pearl streams in the countless host,
Singing to Father, Son, and Holy Ghost:
　　Alleluia! Alleluia!

Lesson 2

Light and Darkness

Are you afraid of the dark? The contrast between light and darkness evokes deep human emotions regarding safety and fear. Darkness is terrifying because we cannot see. Perhaps we cannot see where we are going or what may be lurking out there to harm us. Light, on the other hand, is comforting because with light we can see. We can perceive and understand the lay of the land, and any dangers out there are made clear.

The contrast between light and darkness also evokes the account of creation in Genesis 1. In the darkness that was over the face of the deep, God said, "Let there be light" (Genesis 1:3). God set the sun and the moon in the heavens "to separate the light from the darkness" (Genesis 1:18). God's will for His creation is to have light, to walk in light.

Sin, however, contradicts God's will and plunges the sinner back into darkness. Sin is not merely disobedience; it is a rejection of the Creator and entails a separation from the source of light and life. Therefore, sin ought to be far more terrifying to us than ordinary darkness. How can we live in the light instead of the darkness? John addresses this question in the section we are studying today.

Setting the Stage

John's Letter employs a series of contrasts that form the titles for most of the units in this study. The first of these is the contrast between light and darkness. John associates darkness with sin, while he associates light with God. Like light and darkness, God and sin cannot go together. That is why the forgiveness of sins is absolutely necessary if humanity is to live in fellowship with God.

11. Why does it feel like we are "in the dark" when we sin against God and His Word? What other feelings do we experience when we willingly and knowingly sin?

12. How do you find relief from the guilt of sin?

Confession - turning those feelings over to God - First admit them to myself then tell God

God Is Light

Read 1 John 1:5. There are a handful of passages throughout the Bible that explicitly summarize the Christian message. For example, when Jesus summarizes the message of the Scriptures in Luke 24, he says, "Thus it is written, that the Christ should suffer and on the third day rise from the dead, and that repentance and forgiveness of sins should be proclaimed in His name to all nations" (Luke 24:46–47). In 1 John 1:5, however, John summarizes the message he wants to communicate to his reader as "God is light, and in Him is no darkness at all."

13. What do you think it means to call God "light"? Is this good news or bad news?

Before God all things are revealed - no place to hide

14. Do you think Luke 24:46–47 and 1 John 1:5 are summarizing the same basic message, or are they saying different things? Explain.

Walking in the Light

Read 1 John 1:6–10. "Walking in the light" is another way of saying "being a Christian." At this point in the text, John provides solid instruction about what a Christian life does and does not look like.

15. Which of these people are "walking in the light" as John describes it in verses 6–10?

a. Someone who does not sin.

Only Jesus did that

b. Someone who sins but confesses it.

yes

c. Someone who sins but denies it.

No

16. According to 1 John 1:8, what is the consequence of refusing to confess sins? *The truth is not in us (ie Holy Spirit)*

a. What is the even more severe consequence mentioned in John 1:10? *his word has no place in our lives / Jesus is the Word*

b. If we make God out to be a liar, who are we saying He is like? See John 8:44. *the devil*

17. There are many areas of life in which Christians confess their sins. In which of the following contexts is it easier for us to confess our sins, and in which is it harder? Why?

a. In prayer (as in the Lord's Prayer, for example).

b. At home to our family members against whom we have sinned.

fear that our confession will be used against us

c. In church in the general confession.

d. In private confession with the pastor.

18. What would it take to overcome the barriers to confession that we feel in some of the above contexts?

19. Christ gave the authority to forgive sins to the Church, and that authority is delegated by the congregation to its called pastor. Look up the wording of the absolution in the order of service to which you are most accustomed (*LSB*, p. 151, for example). Is that claim made there? If so, how?

a. Why might such a claim be objectionable to some people? See Mark 2:7.

b. On what basis then can the pastor claim this authority? See John 20:21–23.

c. How is it comforting to have a pastor with this authority?

God's Word for Today

Most religions, and even nonreligious worldviews, have some idea of what people should and should not do, of what it means to walk in the light and to walk in darkness. John, however, gives a uniquely Christian description of these things in the verses we have studied.

20. In what ways do you think Christians today are tempted to "walk in darkness"?

so busy they forget to talk to God keeping up with the "Jonses"

Vilifying those who believe different ie democrats vs republicans

Any activity that pulls us away from God

21. In light of the verses we have studied, offer your own description of what it means to "walk in the light." How is this different from what you may have thought before or from other common views of which you are aware?

In Closing

Encourage participants to begin the following activities:
* Think of the sins that trouble you the most.
* If you are willing, go to your pastor for private confession to be cleansed from all unrighteousness. Remember that the pastor is bound by his ordination vow never to reveal the sins that are confessed to him.
* Next time, if you feel comfortable, describe the experience to others in the group. You need not divulge what you confessed, but you might say something about how you felt about the experience.
* Read 1 John 2:1–17 in preparation for the next session.

Close with prayer. Sing or read in unison the words of "'As Surely As I Live,' God Said" (*LSB* 614). This hymn summarizes the way God has promised to bring forgiveness to the sinner.

"As surely as I live," God said,
"I would not see the sinner dead.
I want him turned from error's ways,
Repentant, living endless days."

And so our Lord gave this command:
"Go forth and preach in ev'ry land;
Bestow on all My pard'ning grace
Who will repent and mend their ways.

"All those whose sins you thus remit
I truly pardon and acquit,

And those whose sins you will retain
Condemned and guilty shall remain.

"What you will bind, that bound shall be;
What you will loose, that shall be free;
To My dear Church the keys are giv'n
To open, close the gates of heav'n."

The words which absolution give
Are His who died that we might live;
The minister whom Christ has sent
Is but His humble instrument.

When ministers lay on their hands,
Absolved by Christ the sinner stands;
He who by grace the Word believes
The purchase of His blood receives.

All praise to You, O Christ, shall be
For absolution full and free,
In which You show Your richest grace;
From false indulgence guard our race.

Praise God the Father and the Son
And Holy Spirit, Three in One,
As was, is now, and so shall be
World without end, eternally!

Lesson 3

Love and Hate

When asked which commandment was the greatest, Jesus pointed to the commands to love God and our neighbor (Matthew 22:34–40). The entire Law, then, can be summarized in one word: *love* (see Romans 13:8–10). In the verses under our consideration this session, John develops the idea that love is the fulfillment of the Law.

In one sense, love is a demand on us. We keep God's commands by loving God and our neighbor. When we fail to love, we sin. However, love can also refer to God's love for us. In this sense, love is a sheer gift. God does not love us because He sees something attractive or lovable in us. He loves us because *He* is love, and He gave His Son as the sacrifice to forgive our sins. Both kinds of love are in play in John's discussion.

Setting the Stage

The status of God's Law was the subject of much contention in the Church during the first century. Some insisted that Christians had to keep all Old Testament laws in order to be saved. Against this position, Paul taught that God's Law (summarized by the Ten Commandments) was still good and applicable to the Christian (Romans 7). However, he also taught that salvation comes through faith in Jesus Christ, not by keeping the Law (Romans 3). Others, like the Gnostics, held that the entire Old Testament was irrelevant to the Christian and that no moral law, much less the Ten Commandments, was binding on the Christian. This is perhaps the position of John's opponents. At any rate, John's opponents seem to claim they can know God without keeping His Commandments.

22. What are some ways that people today try to know God?

Meditation - Mysticism
New Age - Cults -

23. Do you think people today understand God's Law to be binding on them? *No*

Jesus, the Propitiation for Our Sins

Read 1 John 2:1–2. John tells his readers that he does not want them to sin, but God has made a provision for them if they do.

24. Jesus is our "advocate with the Father," which is basically a lawyer for the defense. When Jesus argues your case before the Father, what do you think He says?

"I have already pd the price for her sins"

25. Jesus is the "propitiation for our sins." A propitiation is a sacrifice that puts away God's wrath over sin. Do you think this helps someone who is trying to avoid sin or encourages him or her to sin all the more? Explain your answer.

helps- allows you to forgive yourself & keep trying A hardened heart will use this to justify sinning

Lying and Telling the Truth

Read 1 John 2:3–6. John stresses the importance of integrity by introducing another contrasting pair of concepts: lying and telling the truth. Lying means your actions do not match what you claim about your relationship to God. Telling the truth means they do.

26. How do you know whether you have come to know God and are in Him?

Trust in Him + I believe what the Bible says

And I try to follow his word

27. Does this mean that John thinks his readers do not sin? See 1 John 1:10 and 1 John 2:1.

No

28. When John says that the "love of God" (2:5) is perfected in one who keeps the Commandments, do you think he is referring to our love for God or God's love for us? What difference does it make?

Love: A Command Both Old and New

Read 1 John 2:7–8. John says that he is writing a command that is old and new. This language evokes the "new command" that Jesus gave on Maundy Thursday, that His disciples should love one another.

29. In what sense is the command to love one another an old command? See Leviticus 19:18.

Love your neighbor as yourself

30. In what sense is the command new? See John 13:34–35.

Jesus was the perfect example of love

31. How does Jesus change your understanding of what it means to love?

Willing to sacrifice all

Hate: A Life in Darkness

Read 1 John 2:9–11. In these verses, John further explains the theme of light and darkness, which we explored in the last lesson, by correlating light with love and darkness with hate. Those who hate their brothers stumble because they are in the darkness and cannot see where they are going.

32. Can you think of examples in your life where hate blinded and caused someone to stumble? If so, and if you feel comfortable, share those now.

Supposed Christians hating Trump & all republicans

33. What is the best way to address hate, either in your own heart or the hearts of others?

Hate harms the soul of the hater

Do Not Love the World

Read 1 John 2:15–17. Love is good, but not when directed toward the wrong object. We are to love God and our brother, but not the world or things in the world.

34. When John says, "Do not love the world," what does he mean by "world"?

anything that draws our attention away from God & His will

35. Does this mean that God's creation is evil? Why or why not?

sin has tainted all creation

God's Word for Today

John's polar opposition between light and darkness, love and hate, lying and telling the truth leaves no room for seeing ourselves as partly holy and partly sinful. This may make us uncomfortable if we are accustomed to placing ourselves in some middle position between the two.

36. Do you keep the Commandments? On what basis can you say this?

37. On what basis can you be sure that you know the Father?

In Closing

Encourage participants to begin the following activities:
- If participants would like to share their experience of Confession and Absolution, let them do so.
- Consult a reputable Bible dictionary or other resource to learn more about the word *propitiation*. How does this knowledge help you understand Christ's death on the cross?
- Read 1 John 2:18–27 in preparation for the next session.

Close with prayer. Sing or read the words of "Love Divine, All Love Excelling" (*LSB* 700). This hymn points us to the source of love.

Love divine, all loves excelling,
  Joy of heav'n, to earth come down!
Fix in us Thy humble dwelling,
  All Thy faithful mercies crown.
Jesus, Thou art all compassion,
  Pure, unbounded love Thou art;
Visit us with Thy salvation,
  Enter ev'ry trembling heart.

Breathe, O breathe Thy loving Spirit
    Into ev'ry troubled breast;
Let us all in Thee inherit;
    Let us find Thy promised rest.
Take away the love of sinning;
    Alpha and Omega be;
End of faith, as its beginning,
    Set our hearts at liberty.

Come, Almighty, to deliver;
    Let us all Thy life receive;
Suddenly return, and never,
    Nevermore Thy temples leave.
Thee we would be always blessing,
    Serve Thee as Thy hosts above,
Pray and praise Thee without ceasing,
    Glory in Thy perfect love.

Finish then Thy new creation,
    Pure and spotless let us be;
Let us see Thy great salvation
    Perfectly restored in Thee,
Changed from glory into glory,
    Till in heav'n we take our place,
Till we cast our crowns before Thee,
    Lost in wonder, love, and praise!

Lesson 4

Christ and Antichrists

Perhaps no word in the English language conjures up the image of supreme evil more than the word *Antichrist*. In film, the Antichrist is often portrayed as an attractive and powerful figure, who comes into the world to overthrow all that is good and bring the world to destruction. He is not merely a false teacher, in this view, but is actually a child of Satan, often coming into the world in a way that mirrors Jesus' own virgin birth.

In order to understand the word *antichrist*, however, we first need to understand the word *Christ*. Christ is the Greek equivalent of the Hebrew term *Messiah*, which means "the Anointed One." In the Old Testament, God promised that His Anointed One would deliver His people. For instance, Psalm 2 speaks of the kings of the earth conspiring "against the LORD and against His anointed" (v. 2). However, the Lord tells the Anointed One, "You are My Son" (v. 7) and promises that His Son will rule the nations (v. 8). When Jesus was baptized, He was identified as this same Anointed One when the voice from heaven said, "You are My beloved Son" (Mark 1:11). Jesus, then, is the Christ, because God the Father anointed Him with the Holy Spirit at His Baptism to carry out His mission of saving the world.

Therefore, *antichrist* simply means one who is opposed to the Christ and therefore to His anointing and mission. As we shall see, there are a number of people who merit this title. The Holy Spirit works through the message the apostles received from Christ. Anyone who opposes this message can be called an antichrist.

Setting the Stage

John warns his readers about the coming of the Antichrist, and indeed of many antichrists. These are people who were associated with the Church but "went out from us" (1 John 2:19). The purpose of this section of John's Epistle is to tell his readers how to recognize antichrists. He also want to assure them that the truth they have is the ultimate truth, so they do not need to listen to anyone who claims to have more lofty knowledge than what they have already been taught.

38. What comes to your mind when you hear the word *antichrist*?

39. What beliefs do you expect the Antichrist to promote?

reliance on self - materialistic, having power over others - lusting after power need to liked & feel needed - greedy

The Coming of the Antichrist(s)

Read 1 John 2:18–25. In some places in Scripture, the coming of one Antichrist is predicted. For example, Paul warns of the "man of lawlessness" (2 Thessalonians 2:3–4). John mentions the Antichrist as well, but he also refers to the coming of many antichrists. Antichrist, then, can refer specifically to the one figure of ultimate evil or generally to anyone who opposes Christ. John focuses on the latter sense.

40. According to these verses, what identifies people as antichrists? *they deny that Jesus is the Christ, all unbelievers?*

41. How is this description different than the way people normally imagine the antichrist?

We usually think of them as evil rather than those who refuse to believe

The Anointing

Read 1 John 2:20–21, 24–27. Like later Gnostics, John's opponents seemed to have claimed a secret knowledge, which they believed ordinary Christians lacked. John told his readers that they already had all knowledge because of their anointing by the Holy Spirit. John did not imagine that the Spirit would lead his readers into new, unbiblical truths. He told them, "Let what you heard from the beginning abide in you" (1 John 2:24). The teaching activity of the Spirit cannot be separated from the message John received from Christ and gave to his readers.

Anoint means to pour oil on someone. In the Old Testament, this action designated someone as a king or a prophet. But one can also be anointed by the Holy Spirit, as Jesus was at His Baptism. John informed his readers that they, too, had been anointed by the Spirit. Early baptismal liturgies often included anointing with oil (called chrismation), along with the baptizing in water, to correspond ritually to the coming of the Holy Spirit at Baptism. Through the coming of the Spirit, the baptismal candidates became, as Luther said, "little Christs."

The antichrists, then, are opposed not only to Jesus and His anointing but also to the Christians and their anointing.

42. John says that his readers have "no need that anyone should teach you" (1 John 2:27). Do you think John understands himself to be teaching his readers? Explain.

Only to reinforce what they were first taught - the gospel!

43. Do you think John means there should be no teachers at all in the Church?

no, but they need to teach only what the Bible says

44. In what sense do you need a teacher?

to figure out how to apply it to God's word to my everyday life

45. In what sense do you *not* need a teacher?

God's Word for Today

John addressed a particular problem in the Church of his day: false teachers (antichrists), who were opposing Christ and insisting that they had the true teaching. John directs Christians to have confidence in their own anointing with the Spirit through what they learned from the beginning. How do these things apply to our situation today?

46. Do you recognize any antichrists today? Who are they?

Mormons - or any group that has secret teaching not available to the public

47. If someone claims that he or she is led by the Spirit to a particular belief, how can you discern whether that claim is true? -

do they proclaim Jesus as the Christ

In Closing

Encourage participants to begin the following activities:
- Read 2 Thessalonians 2:1–12 to gain more information about the Antichrist. How does this compare to John's presentation of this topic?
- Consult a reputable Bible dictionary or other source to learn about the practice of anointing.
- Read 1 John 2:28–3:10 in preparation for the next session.

Close with prayer. Sing or read the words of "Lord, Keep Us Steadfast in Your Word" (*LSB* 655). This hymn is a prayer for protection against all enemies of Christ.

> Lord, keep us steadfast in Your Word;
> Curb those who by deceit or sword
> Would wrest the kingdom from Your Son
> And bring to naught all He has done.

> Lord Jesus Christ, Your pow'r make known,
> For You are Lord of lords alone;
> Defend Your holy Church that we
> May sing Your praise eternally.

> O Comforter of priceless worth,
> Send peace and unity on earth;
> Support us in our final strife
> And lead us out of death to life.

Lesson 5

Children of God; Children of the Devil

In our verses for today, John appears to operate with the assumption "Like father, like son." In other words, children tend to behave like their parents. This is true not only in ordinary human families but also in the family of God. Children of God behave like God, and children of the devil behave like the devil.

In principle, this means that all the stark contrasts John rehearses in his Letter, such as light/darkness, truth/lie, love/hate, also correspond to the lives of his readers. Those who are children of the devil live lives characterized by darkness, lies, and hate, while those who are children of God live lives of light, truth, and love.

John is not saying that the lives of unbelievers are always evil in an obvious way. Certainly, we recognize that unbelievers are often good neighbors, good citizens, and the like. This idea is affirmed in the Scriptures (see Romans 2:14–15). John, however, is speaking of the basic orientation of our lives, which can either be toward God or toward the devil. This orientation is what lies beneath our daily activities.

Setting the Stage

As we saw in the previous lessons, John leaves no room for us to imagine ourselves halfway between sin and holiness: "No one who abides in Him keeps on sinning" (1 John 3:6). Texts like this raise the question of whether we must be perfect in this life in order to be Christians. This question will engage us in the study, but for now we should note that it is no surprise that John describes the Christian life in terms of a stark contrast between sin and holiness since his entire Letter is structured around stark contrasts.

48. Why do you think some Christians believe they can live their lives without sinning? What is attractive about this false belief?

Whatever they do is right - no matter how much it hurts others. They think they are better than others - no guilt

49. How should Christians react to God's unceasing demand for perfection?

reliance on God's love to wash away our sin - We can come to Him without fear & admit our sins

The Father's Love for Us

Read 1 John 2:28–3:3. In His love for us, God made us His children. This fact transforms our lives. We begin to act like God acts. This not only identifies us as His children, but also it marks us as alien to the world. Just as the antichrists oppose the anointing of Christians because they oppose the anointing of Christ, so also the world does not know Christians because it does not know Christ.

John does not suggest that our behavior now measures up to God's standard of perfection, but he looks forward to the day when Christ will appear. On that day, what we are now by faith will be fully revealed when "we shall be like Him, because we shall see Him as He is" (1 John 3:2).

50. How do these passages illustrate the principle "Like father, like son"?

Just like a child imitates the father So we imitate God & with the HS work in us we become more like Him

51. Even though we are God's children, the devil, the world, and our sinful flesh still fight against us. How do we see that in our everyday lives? Provide practical examples.

Bad language in dreams. -

52. What information do these verses give us about the day when Christ will return? *We will be like him & see him as he is*

53. Read 1 Corinthians 15:50–57 and describe how we will be changed at Christ's return.

perishable → imperishable
mortal → immortal

54. When you think of Christ's return, are you filled with confidence or shame (1 John 2:28)? Why?

relief

55. How does John say you can become pure?

by turning from Sin

The End of Sin

Read 1 John 3:4–10. Sin is lawlessness, but Christ came to take away sin. He takes away sin first by offering Himself as a sacrifice to atone for sins (propitiation). He then strengthens God's children through His Word and Spirit to lead godly lives. Unlike propitiation, which gives us full forgiveness of sins now, Christ's activity in our lives through our good works is not yet perfect.

56. When John states that no one who keeps on sinning has either seen or known Him, is he saying that Christians never sin? See 1 John 1:10. *No but we try to turn from sin with God's help*

57. What is John saying? Note how he phrases it in 1 John 3:4.

58. What is the difference between a Christian who sins and a non-Christian who sins?

repentance & forgiveness

God's Word for Today

John argues strongly that your actions reveal whose child you are. He speaks in absolute contrasts, which will not be fulfilled until the Last Day (see 1 John 3:2–3). Nevertheless, God is at work in our lives now. Because of this, we can draw comfort, not only from God's promise of forgiveness, but also from His activity in our lives now.

59. What evidence do you see in your life that would identify you as God's child?

60. What contrary evidence do you see, and what can be done about it?

In Closing

Encourage participants to begin the following activities:
- Review the Ten Commandments (from Luther's Small Catechism or Exodus 20:1–17) to see the shape of a life lived according to God's design.
- Read Romans 7:7–25, and reflect on how this description of the Christian life compares and contrasts to the one in 1 John.
- Read 1 John 3:11–24 in preparation for the next session.

Close with prayer. Sing or read the words to the hymn "The People That in Darkness Sat" (*LSB* 412). This hymn employs many of the major images in 1 John.

The people that in darkness sat
  A glorious light have seen;
The light has shined on them who long
  In shades of death have been,
  In shades of death have been.

To hail Thee, Sun of Righteousness,
  The gath'ring nations come;
They joy as when the reapers bear
  Their harvest treasures home,
  Their harvest treasures home.

To us a Child of hope is born,
  To us a Son is giv'n,
And on His shoulder ever rests
  All pow'r in earth and heav'n,
  All pow'r in earth and heav'n.

His name shall be the Prince of Peace,
  The Everlasting Lord,
The Wonderful, the Counselor,
  The God by all adored,
  The God by all adored.

His righteous government and pow'r
  Shall over all extend;
On judgment and on justice based,
  His reign shall have no end,
  His reign shall have no end.

Lord Jesus, reign in us, we pray,
  And make us Thine alone.
Who with the Father ever art
  And Holy Spirit, one,
  And Holy Spirit, one.

Lesson 6

Love and Murder

Murder—it is one of the most heinous crimes possible. Those who sit on death row have probably committed murder. John, however, does not limit the word *murder* to those who have physically killed someone. He expands the term to include anyone who hates. He is not merely saying that hatred may lead to murder, but he is saying that hatred itself is in some way equivalent to murder.

It is true that in the sight of human beings, murder and hatred are not the same. Murder destroys life in a way that hatred does not. Murder carries far greater criminal penalties than hatred. Murder evokes more horror than hatred. One would probably rather live next door to a hater than a murderer. Nevertheless, in the sight of God, hatred is no different than murder.

This fundamental insight gives new urgency to the necessity to love. No one wants to live a life entangled and burdened by murder. However, it is no longer possible for people to comfort themselves with the thought that although they may not love as they should, at least they have not committed murder. Although they may not be perfect, at least they are not as bad as a criminal. If the failure to love is tantamount to murder, then love is the only option. There are no excuses. Love is the way of a Christian.

Setting the Stage

In this section, John cycles back around to the theme of love and hate, which we covered in Lesson 3. When John returns to a theme, he not only repeats it, he intensifies it. So here he speaks not merely of hate, but of murder. This is part of a progressive unmasking of sin that John employs throughout his Letter. In 1 John 2:1–11, we saw that anyone who does not keep God's Commandments is a liar, walks in darkness, and hates his brother. Now John calls such a person a murderer.

61. How would you define love?

treating others with kindness & respect helping them when needed

62. How would you define hate?

actively trying to hurt or disrespect someone – being happy when bad things happen to them

The Example of Cain

Read 1 John 3:11–13. When Cain killed Abel, he became the first murderer, the prototype of all killers throughout history. John raises the example of Cain as a warning to his readers that they should not follow in Cain's footsteps. John is concerned, however, not only with the outward act of murder, but also with Cain's inner motivations. If we understand what drove Cain to kill Abel, similar motivations in our own hearts will be unmasked, and we will not so readily follow Cain's example.

63. Read Genesis 4:1–8. According to Genesis, why did Cain kill Abel?

sin was working in his heart

64. How does John describe the reason Cain killed Abel?

his actions were evil + Abel's righteous

65. What evidence is there in the Genesis account to support John's explanation?

Lord looked in favor of Abel but not Cain

What Love Looks Like

Read 1 John 3:14–18. Jesus laid down His life for His brothers, willingly handing Himself over to be murdered. This is the ultimate act of love. Paul goes so far as to say that this self-sacrificial attitude is what it means to have the same mind as Christ (Philippians 2:5–8). This is how we know what love looks like. This act of love did not end with Jesus' death, however. John insists that it opens our hearts and leads us to concrete actions to help those in need.

66. How can we "lay down our lives for the brothers" if we are not being threatened with death?

- going out of our way to help others making a sacrifice

67. Why do you think John equates hate and murder? See Matthew 5:21–22.

both are a state of the heart

68. People today often think of love primarily as a feeling. What do you think John would say about that?

Love is a decision

The Confidence That Love Gives

Read 1 John 3:19–24. In this section, John tells us that our love gives us confidence and reassures our hearts before God. It is easy to see how we can have this confidence once Christ has returned and we are like Him because we see Him as He is (1 John 3:2b). However, as long as "what we will be has not yet appeared" (1 John 3:2a), our love is still corrupted by sin.

69. To what extent does your love reassure your heart before God?

sometimes - but need repentance daily

70. What hope does John give to those who are not reassured by it?

God is greater than our hearts

71. What do you think John would want you to do if you are not reassured? See 1 John 1:8–9.

repent

God's Word for Today

John's discussion of love and murder forces us to think about our lives in ways that perhaps we do not normally think about them. John's stark contrast between love and murder intensifies our duty to love, and it encourages us to think of Jesus as the model of what love looks like.

72. What did you learn about love and murder today that you did not know before? If you feel comfortable, share your thoughts with the group.

73. What are the greatest obstacles to love that you can identify, and how can they be overcome?

fear of being hurt or taken advantage of.

God is in charge!

In Closing

Encourage participants to begin the following activities:
- Make a list of tangible ways you can demonstrate love to others.
- Pick something on the list that you do not normally do, and do it.
- Read 1 John 4:1–6 in preparation for the next session.

Close with prayer. Sing or read the words of "Son of God, Eternal Savior" (*LSB* 842). This hymn is a prayer for Christ to grant, among other things, that we may meet our neighbor's physical needs.

Son of God, eternal Savior,
    Source of life and truth and grace,
Word made flesh, whose birth among us
    Hallows all our human race,
You our Head, who, throned in glory,
    For Your own will ever plead:
Fill us with Your love and pity,
    Heal our wrongs, and help our need.

As You, Lord, have lived for others,
    So may we for others live.
Freely have Your gifts been granted;
    Freely may Your servants give.
Yours the gold and Yours the silver,
    Yours the wealth of land and sea;
We but stewards of Your bounty
    Held in solemn trust will be.

Come, O Christ, and reign among us,
    King of love and Prince of Peace;
Hush the storm of strife and passion,
    Bid its cruel discords cease.
By Your patient years of toiling,
    By Your silent hours of pain,
Quench our fevered thirst of pleasure,
    Stem our selfish greed of gain.

Son of God, eternal Savior,
    Source of life and truth and grace,
Word made flesh, whose birth among us
    Hallows all our human race:
By Your praying, by Your willing
    That Your people should be one,
Grant, O grant our hope's fruition:
    Here on earth Your will be done.

Lesson 7

Spirit of God; Spirit of the Antichrist

The Holy Spirit is indispensable for the life of the Church. We have already seen how John tells his readers that they have an anointing from the Spirit that abides in them and teaches them (1 John 2:26–27). Paul, too, stresses the importance of the Spirit when he calls the Word of God the "sword of the Spirit" (Ephesians 6:17). Jesus Himself promises entrance into the kingdom of God to those who are "born of water and the Spirit" (John 3:5).

Not everything that claims to be spiritual, however, is true. Our world is full of a bewildering variety of claims about spirits and the Holy Spirit. If you do a quick scan of programs on television or resources on the Web, you will likely find claims about ghosts, communication with the dead, advice on how to get in touch with your spirit, as well as special teachings supposedly given by the Holy Spirit. Some of these claims present themselves as compatible with Christianity, and some do not. So how is a Christian, who believes in the reality of the Holy Spirit and of angels, supposed to make sense of these contradictory and confusing messages? In this lesson, John gives advice on how to "test the spirits."

Setting the Stage

John has already dealt with the topic of Christ and antichrists (see Lesson 4, 1 John 2:18–27). Now he returns to the same theme, but he shifts the focus from Christ to the Holy Spirit. Previously, John referred to all who denied that Jesus was the Christ as antichrists (1 John 2:22). Now he tracks the root error a step further back. He considers not only the person who denies Christ, but also the spirit who motivates that denial. This, he says, is the spirit of the antichrist (1 John 4:3).

More generally, John's discussion raises once again the question of truth versus error. He treats this issue as he treats all other issues by using stark contrasts. One's confession is either from the Spirit of God or the spirit of the antichrist. There is no middle position, nor is there room for a superficial humility that would claim that all religions have a piece of the truth.

74. What claims have you heard that are presented as coming from the Spirit? *Celebrate Diversity ie homosexuality Welcome all the emmigrants & ie its okay to break the law There are many paths to God (Heaven)*

75. On what basis do you normally evaluate such claims?

What does God say in the Bible.
1) homosexuality is wrong
2) We are to obey civil authority unless it disobeys God

Testing the Spirits

Read 1 John 4:1–3. Contradictory claims of truth revealed by the Spirit are nothing new in history. As we shall see, God's people had to contend with these claims in both the Old and New Testaments. John's instructions about testing the Spirit focus on what a particular message confesses about Christ. We have already seen that John's opponents claimed to be without sin (1 John 1:8) and denied that Jesus is the Christ (1 John 2:22). In these verses, however, John sharpens his criteria for testing the spirits by making Jesus' incarnation the touchstone of whether a given confession arises from the Spirit of God or the spirit of the antichrist.

This is not the only criterion for testing spirits in the Scriptures, however. We can gain a more complete understanding of the issues involved by looking at passages in other parts of God's Word.

76. What criteria for testing the spirits are listed or depicted in the following passages?

a. Deuteronomy 18:20–22

Prophacy Not Coming true

b. Deuteronomy 13:1–3

Calls to worship other Gods

c. Matthew 16:13–23

Confess Jesus is Christ

d. Galatians 1:8

Only the true Gospel

e. 1 Corinthians 12:3

Say "Jesus is Lord" only by the HS

77. Taking these passages together with those we have reviewed in this section, how would you describe a comprehensive scriptural way of testing the spirits?

Do they add or delete anything from the true Gospel?

When you compare 1 John 4:3 with the other criteria listed in Scripture, the unique element in 1 John is that the Spirit of God confesses that "Jesus Christ has come in the flesh" (4:2). John focuses on this criterion, it seems, because that is the heart of his opponents' error. They may well have taught, like later Gnostics, that Jesus was a normal human being, but that a spirit being called "Christ" descended on Him at His Baptism. This "Christ" later departed from Jesus before His crucifixion, or so they maintained.

78. What religious claims have you heard that would deny that Jesus Christ has come in the flesh?

Overcoming the World

Read 1 John 4:4–6. In 1 John, the "world" is a fearful place. By "world" John does not mean God's good creation. He means the fallen creation that is captive to darkness, hate, and murder. He means those who speak the words of the antichrist and the devil. However, as John tells his readers, Christians have already overcome those who are from the world. These forces are no reason for a Christian to lose hope. We Christians have this victory, not because we are greater than those in the world, but because "He who is in you is greater than he who is in the world" (1 John 4:4).

79. How does John's description of life as a combat between "He who is in you" and "he who is in the world" give meaning to the daily tasks of your life? How does it give you comfort?

We need to be constantly on alert. The HS must be our guide & security system

80. John assumes that a message from the world will be more popular than a message from God, because that is what the world wants to hear. What do you think are the most popular false messages in our world today?

Every one else is doing it.

God's Word for Today

Sometimes when Christians want to depart from a clear teaching in the Scriptures, they claim that the Spirit is revealing something new in the church. For example, Scripture clearly prohibits homosexual activity (Romans 1:26–27), yet one bishop in a major Protestant denomination said in a sermon that God was doing a "new thing" in the Church by showing that homosexuality was a "state of being," not a transgression of God's Law.[1] We can use this claim as a case study for "testing the spirits" today.

---

[1] http://www.umaffirm.org/gcnews5.html. Sermon by United Methodist Bishop Jack M. Tuell, preached in Des Moines, Washington. Accessed August 15, 2008.

81. Using what you learned in this lesson, how would you evaluate the claim of this sermon?

God's word does not change –
He says homosexual activity is wrong

82. Elsewhere, the sermon argues Christians should accept homosexuality as a God-given identity because of God's inclusive love for all of humanity (John 3:16), which is the central message of Scripture. How does what you have learned about God's love and light in previous lessons help you to respond to this argument? (See especially 1 John 3:18–24; 1:5–10.)

God does not love our sin – he
loves us + hates our sin – We
must seperate the person + the sin

In Closing

Encourage participants to begin the following activities:
- Skim the Book of Galatians, and make a list of the false positions that Paul combats there.
- Compare and contrast those positions with the false positions that John contends against in 1 John.
- Read 1 John 4:7–21 in preparation for the next session.

Close with prayer. Sing or read the words of "Holy Spirit, Ever Dwelling" (*LSB* 650).

Holy Spirit, ever dwelling
   In the holiest realms of light;
Holy Spirit, ever brooding
   O'er a world of gloom and night;
Holy Spirit, ever raising
   Those of earth to thrones on high;
Living, life-imparting Spirit,
   You we praise and magnify.

Holy Spirit, ever living
   As the Church's very life;
Holy Spirit, ever striving
   Through us in a ceaseless strife;
Holy Spirit, ever forming
   In the Church the mind of Christ:
You we praise with endless worship
   For Your gifts and fruits unpriced.

Holy Spirit, ever working
   Through the Church's ministry;
Quick'ning, strength'ning, and absolving,
   Setting captive sinners free;
Holy Spirit, ever binding
   Age to age and soul to soul
In communion never ending,
   You we worship and extol.

Lesson 8

Love and Fear

God strikes fear into the human heart. When God was about to give the Ten Commandments on Mount Sinai, for example, the people were terrified because the mountain was wrapped in smoke. They saw lightning and heard peals of thunder and a trumpet blast (Exodus 19:16–20). God has been known to kill the disobedient on the spot (see Leviticus 10:1–2; Acts 5:1–11). Ultimately, God promises to punish sinners in hell (Matthew 10:28).

Nevertheless, it is also true that the entire Bible can be summarized as a story of God's love for His people. God's people were continually unfaithful, but God remained faithful and committed to them. This faithfulness and love toward His people unfolded as God brought the Israelites out of slavery in Egypt, kept them alive in the desert, and brought them to the Promised Land. It culminated in God's sending His Son to die for the sins of the world.

So which experience of God is ultimately decisive for our lives? Fear or love? There is good scriptural foundation for both reactions to God, but John tells us in the verses before us today that love has the last word.

Setting the Stage

In previous sections of his Epistle, John tells us that we are to love, not hate, our neighbor (1 John 2:7–11) and that we are to love one another rather than follow the murderous example of Cain (1 John 3:11–15). Now he shifts the focus from our relation to our neighbor to our relation to God. That relationship, he says, should be characterized by love (first and foremost God's love toward us) and not fear. Only in this way can our relation to our neighbor be one of love and not hate.

83. If you feel comfortable, describe times that you have loved God and times that you have been afraid of Him.

84. Do you find that your attitude toward God affects your attitude toward your neighbor? Explain.

When my Trust in God & his love is strong, it is easier to show love to others

God's Love for Us

Read 1 John 4:7–12. We find it easier to love people who love us first. Because of this, we may be tempted to think that God works the same way and that His love for us is really motivated by our love for Him. John, however, tells us that it is precisely the other way around. God loved us first. We did nothing to bring about that love.

85. Read verse 9. This is the ultimate picture of what love looks like. Reflect on this verse for a few minutes, and make a list of at least three characteristics of God's love that you can derive from it. Compare and contrast these characteristics with ordinary human love.

God sacrificed his most valuable possession - a piece of himself maybe not a piece but the whole. Selfless, Visible, Gives life

86. Read verse 10. God's love not only has these three characteristics, but also it is directed toward people who do not love Him. How does this fact change the way you estimate your own worth and that of others?

We all have great worth in God's eyes, whether rich or poor, clean or dirty

87. Read verses 11–12. In his Gospel, John also points out that "no one has ever seen God." Read John 1:18 and compare it to 1 John 4:11–12. How does God make Himself visible? Do you think these passages contradict each other? Explain.

Jesus made God known to us

Perfect Love Casts Out Fear

Read 1 John 4:13–21. The work of the three persons of the Trinity is evident in these verses. Out of love, God the Father sends His Son to be the Savior of the world. He also gives us of His Spirit as a pledge that we abide in Him and He in us. Since God is love, this means that we abide in His love, and His love abides in us. All of this gives us the confidence to stand before Him without fear on Judgment Day.

88. As you contemplate Judgment Day, what sources of fear do you find in yourself?

fear of my evil deeds being exposed to all
fear of seeing those I love not saved

89. John says that we can have confidence on Judgment Day "because as He is so also are we in this world" (v. 17). How can we be secure in God's love, knowing that day is coming?

Trust - based on prior experiences

90. Look at verse 18. In Luther's Small Catechism, the explanations of most of the Commandments begin, "We should fear and love God so that . . . " How is this consistent with what John says in this verse?

Two different types of fear.
1- respect
2- punishment

God's Word for Today

Though God certainly threatens to punish sin, His ultimate will is to inspire love in our hearts, not fear. This fact has many implications for our worship and our lives. Someone who relates to God primarily out of fear will exhibit different attitudes and behaviors than someone who relates to God primarily on the basis of God's love.

91. People can go to church out of fear or out of love. How would someone motivated by fear describe the benefit of going to church? someone motivated by love?

fire & brimstone – have to go
love – want to go

92. People can put in an honest day's work out of fear or out of love. What would someone motivated by fear hope to gain from this honesty? someone motivated by love?

fear – exhausted
love – energized tho physically tired

In Closing

Encourage participants to begin the following activities:
- Review Luther's explanations of the Ten Commandments in the Small Catechism.
- Read 1 Corinthians 13, the most famous chapter about love in the Bible. Compare and contrast what Paul has to say about love with what we have learned from John.
- Read 1 John 5:1–12 in preparation for the next session.

Close with prayer. Read or sing the words of "Oh, How Great Is Your Compassion" (*LSB* 559). This hymn praises God for His trinitarian work of salvation, picking up many of the themes found in this section of 1 John.

Oh, how great is Your compassion,
　Faithful Father, God of grace,
　That with all our fallen race

In our depth of degradation
　　You had mercy so that we
　　Might be saved eternally!

Your great love for this has striven
　　That we may, from sin made free,
　　Live with You eternally.
Your dear Son Himself has given
　　And extends His gracious call,
　　To His supper leads us all.

Firmly to our soul's salvation
　　Witnesses Your Spirit, Lord,
　　In Your Sacraments and Word.
There He sends true consolation,
　　Giving us the gift of faith
　　That we fear not hell nor death.

Lord, Your mercy will not leave me;
　　Ever will Your truth abide.
　　Then in You I will confide.
Since Your Word cannot deceive me,
　　My salvation is to me
　　Safe and sure eternally.

I will praise Your great compassion,
　　Faithful Father, God of grace,
　　That with all our fallen race
In our depth of degradation
　　You had mercy so that we
　　Might be saved eternally.

Lesson 9

Faith

All human beings have faith in something. In his Large Catechism, Luther teaches that whatever one has faith in is one's "god," whether that is a pagan idol, money, learning, or anything else. In our day, some people feel that their life has no meaning unless they are in a romantic relationship. They have made relationships their god because that is where they find comfort and security. Still others measure their worth and gain their identity from their careers. For them, their career is their god. Even atheists who argue that all religion is irrational have a god in a sense. They have made human reason their god because they find in it the source of their confidence.

For Luther, however, the heart and soul of Christianity is that we look to the true God for all good things and to no other source. That is what it means to have faith. That is why Luther insisted that salvation is by faith alone. That is another way of saying that all our hope and confidence are in Christ and what He has done for us, not in our own efforts at pleasing God. For Luther, the most subtle false god is our own good works. Good works are, in fact, good and are commanded by God, but when they become the source of our confidence before God, they usurp Christ's role as our Savior; they themselves become our god. In a simple way, John speaks of both faith and works in this section, showing us how they should relate to each other.

Setting the Stage

Earlier in his Epistle, John made the point that we are God's children because of the love He has given us (1 John 3:1). In this section, John returns to this theme but adds another dimension to what it means to be God's child: faith. God's children believe that Jesus is

53

the Christ. Faith in Jesus not only makes us God's children, but also it makes God's commands a delight and it overcomes the world.

However, faith does not exist in a vacuum. Faith is based on testimony. From the very beginning of his First Epistle, John tells us that he is giving us eyewitness testimony (1 John 1:1–3). Now he fills out the details of his testimony by saying (somewhat cryptically) that the Spirit, the water, and the blood testify. We will explore the meaning of this statement in this lesson.

93. In your own words, describe what it means to believe that Jesus is the Christ. You may wish to review Lesson 4.

believe that Jesus is the son of God + that he died on the cross for my sins + he rose on the 3rd day

94. What events in Jesus' life do you think most clearly indicate that He is the Christ?

his resurrection

Faith and Works

Read 1 John 5:1–5. We noted in Lesson 3 that love is the fulfillment of the Law, and as such it is a demand God places on the Christian. When John introduces faith into the discussion, however, love seems to lose its character as a demand and take on a new character as something joyful and free.

95. Look at 1 John 5:3; then read Romans 7:7–25. Which passage better describes your experience of God's Law? Explain.

I struggle every day with my sinful nature.

96. When John says that God's commands are not burdensome, he echoes the words of Jesus. How does Matthew 11:28–30 help us understand why God's commands are not burdensome?

We can take our struggles to Jesus

54

97. Faith overcomes God's wrath by trusting in Jesus for the forgiveness of sins, but how does faith overcome the world?

God overcame the world thru Jesus death & resurrection

The Spirit, the Water, and the Blood

Read 1 John 5:6–12. John says that the Spirit, the water, and the blood testify that Jesus is the Christ. However, to what these three refer is not immediately clear. We can gain a deeper understanding of this passage by pondering events in Jesus' life in which the Spirit, water, or blood is key.

98. Briefly note the way in which the Spirit, water, or blood figures in the following events of Jesus' life:

a. Jesus' Baptism (John 1:29–34)

John baptizes Jesus in water & the Spirit descends on Him

b. Jesus turns water into wine (John 2:1–11)

miracle of turning water into wine

c. Jesus' side is pierced (John 19:34–35)

blood & water flow from his side

99. Pick the event that you think most clearly testifies that Jesus is the Christ (the Anointed One), and describe how the Spirit, the water, or the blood testifies to this.

100. Identify the way in which the Spirit, the water, and the blood continue to testify in the Church today according to the following passages:

a. John 20:21–23 (Spirit)

We are given the Spirit to give us faith

b. John 3:5 (water)

Born in the water of baptism

c. John 6:53–55 (blood)

Dine on the flesh & blood of Christ thru the Holy Supper

55

God's Word for Today

In the text for today, John gives us the testimony that forms the basis of our faith in Christ, and he spells out the victory that faith brings. This testimony and this faith bring us eternal life. For this reason, they also give us a new perspective on our daily lives.

101. Pick one aspect of your daily life, and describe how what you have learned about faith changes the way you view it.

102. How would your daily routine be different if you did not have faith?

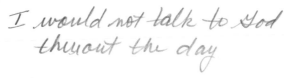

I would not talk to God thruout the day

In Closing

Encourage participants to begin the following activities:
- Read Luther's explanation of the First Commandment in the Large Catechism. This is where Luther defines what it means to have faith.
- Look through any setting of the liturgy in your hymnal, and identify references to the Spirit, water, or blood.
- Read 1 John 5:13–21 in preparation for the next session.

Close with prayer. Sing or read the words of "Water, Blood, and Spirit Crying" (*LSB* 597). Note how the hymn interprets these three items from 1 John 5:8.

Water, blood, and Spirit crying,
By their witness testifying
To the One whose death-defying
    Life has come, with life for all.

In a wat'ry grave are buried
All our sins that Jesus carried;

Christ, the Ark of Life, has ferried
   Us across death's raging flood.

Dark the way, yet Christ precedes us,
Past the scowl of death He leads us;
Spreads a table where He feeds us
   With His body and His blood.

Though around us death is seething,
God, His two-edged sword unsheathing,
By His Spirit life is breathing
   Through the living, active Word.

Spirit, water, blood entreating,
Working faith and its completing
In the One whose death-defeating
   Life has come, with life for all.

Lesson 10

Prayer

In *The Devil's Dictionary*, American satirist Ambrose Bierce (1842–1914?) defined "pray" as follows: "PRAY, v. To ask that the laws of the universe be annulled in behalf of a single petitioner confessedly unworthy." There is a kernel of truth to this irreverent definition of prayer. Does it not seem rather presumptuous of us to approach God's throne and present our requests? Who are we to think that we could gain a hearing from the King of heaven?

Luther, too, was aware of this difficulty. In fact, in his Large Catechism, he raises the issue of people who use this difficulty as an excuse not to pray. Luther tells us that we should not say to ourselves, "I am not holy or worthy enough. If I were as godly and holy as St. Peter or St. Paul, then I would pray" (*Concordia*, p. 410). Instead, Luther tells us we should take a different attitude: "Here I come, dear Father, and pray, not because of my own purpose or because of my own worthiness. But I pray because of Your commandment and promise, which cannot fail or deceive me" (ibid.).

In the reading for today, John addresses the same issue by stressing Christ's promise to hear our prayer. He then turns his attention specifically to prayer for brothers and sisters who commit sin. In some cases, we should pray for them; in other cases, not. He then closes his Epistle with the promise of eternal life and the exhortation to stay away from idols.

Setting the Stage

Here at the end of his Epistle, John returns to a theme he brought up at the beginning: the word of life (see 1 John 1:1). He says that his purpose in writing is that "you may know that you have eternal life"

(1 John 5:13). As usual, however, John does not merely repeat a theme; he develops it further. Because we have eternal life in Christ, we also have the confidence that He hears our prayers and grants us what we ask in His name. This section then is a mini-manual on how to pray and what to pray for.

103. What kinds of things do you pray for? What kind of things do you feel uncomfortable praying for?

healing for friends & family relief from stress or sickness or depression Guidance - wisdom

No - winning a game or drawing

104. In your experience, what attitudes or habits get in the way of prayer?

Allow myself to get too busy or distracted Believing what God's answer is going to be why pray

Christ's Promise concerning Prayer

Read 1 John 5:13–15. In these verses, John argues from the greater to the lesser. If God has given us eternal life in Christ, He surely also is concerned to hear and grant our prayer. This promise is a prominent theme in the Scriptures. Yet it is also possible for the promise to provoke a sense of anxiety in the Christian. What happens if I pray and nothing happens?

105. Along with 1 John 5:14–15, read the following Scripture passages. In your own words, summarize what Christ promises about prayer.

a. John 14:13–14

Ask for anything

b. Matthew 7:7

ask + receive

In the Lord's Prayer, Jesus tells us to pray "Thy will be done." In 1 John 5:14, John says that our prayer should be "according to His will." However, some Christians insist that we should not include that qualifier "if it be Your will" in our prayers because this shows a lack of faith. We should instead assume that God will grant us exactly what we ask for, they say, whether it be health or wealth or anything else. Often the promises cited in the previous question are brought forward as evidence for this position.

106. How would you respond to this objection? If you admit to yourself the possibility that God might not give you exactly what you ask for, are you showing a lack of faith? You may wish to consider the example of the three men in the fiery furnace (Daniel 3:16–18).

I don't always know what is best for me or for others So I ask for God's will so that my prayer doesn't mess things up.

Sin That Leads to Death

Read 1 John 5:16–18. John encourages his readers to pray for fellow Christians who commit sin. However, he does not suggest that we should pray for those who commit sin that leads to death. However, John doesn't define what that sin is. Nevertheless, we can gain some insight by comparing John's words with Jesus' words in Matthew.

Read Matthew 12:31–32. The Pharisees had said that Jesus casts out demons by the prince of demons. In effect, they were saying that a work Christ performed by the power of the Holy Spirit was, in fact, performed by the devil. In response, Jesus says that the blasphemy against the Holy Spirit will not be forgiven.

107. Read 1 John 1:8–10. How is claiming we have not sinned similar to Jesus' description of the blasphemy against the Holy Spirit? What does each say about God?

That God is a liar & not all powerful

108. How would you describe sin that does not lead to death? How is it different from sin that leads to death?

Sin that leads to death is unbelief All other sins can be forgiven

Conclusion

Read 1 John 5:19–21. At the end of his Epistle, John traces the stark contrasts he has employed throughout the Letter back to their origins: God and the devil. We are from God, he says, but "the whole world lies in the power of the evil one" (v. 19).

109. Summarize from your recollection of 1 John the characteristics of the world and the characteristics of God.

God = truth, love, light

World = lies, hate, darkness (shadow)

110. How does John's description of God and the world help you to think of your own life differently than you have before?

God's Word for Today

Prayer is the culmination of all that God has done for our salvation. He sent His Son to give us true understanding and eternal life. He has also promised to hear our prayer and grant us anything we ask according to His will. Therefore, it is only natural that we pray for God's life to extend to others as well.

111. How often do you pray that God would grant life to a specific person?

not as often as I should

112. How does what you have learned about prayer encourage you to make use of this privilege?

All prayer is answered

In Closing

Encourage participants to begin the following activities:
- Read Jesus' instructions about prayer in Matthew 6:5–15.
- Read Luther's explanation of the Lord's Prayer in the Large Catechism.
- Read 2 and 3 John in preparation for the next session.

Close with prayer. Sing or read the words of "To God the Holy Spirit Let Us Pray" (*LSB* 768).

To God the Holy Spirit let us pray
For the true faith needed on our way
That He may defend us when life is ending
And from exile home we are wending.
    Lord, have mercy!

O sweetest Love, Your grace on us bestow;
Set our hearts with sacred fire aglow
That with hearts united we love each other,
Ev'ry stranger, sister, and brother.
    Lord, have mercy!

Transcendent Comfort in our ev'ry need,
Help us neither scorn nor death to heed
That we may not falter nor courage fail us
When the foe shall taunt and assail us.
    Lord, have mercy!

Shine in our hearts, O Spirit, precious light;
Teach us Jesus Christ to know aright
That we may abide in the Lord who bought us,
Till to our true home He has brought us.
    Lord, have mercy!

Lesson 11

2 and 3 John

The next two Epistles of John, especially 2 John, may be viewed as miniature versions of 1 John. They pick many of the same themes John deals with in his First Epistle: love, God's Commandments, anti-christs, abiding in the teaching of Christ, testimony to the truth. Of these themes, the two most prominent are love and truth.

However, at least in our society, it is not immediately apparent that love and truth are compatible. Love is often viewed as synonymous with acceptance and toleration. Therefore, any insistence on truth tends to be seen as narrow and exclusive. This can be the case even in the Church, where an insistence on pure doctrine is sometimes seen as "unloving." It might appear that one must choose between truth and love.

John, however, insists on both. In 2 John, he returns to the commandment of love, which he says his readers have had from the beginning. But he also insists that those who do not abide in the teaching of Christ do not have God. In 3 John, he commends Gaius for his love, but he also says that what brings him the greatest joy is that his children are walking in the truth. These two Epistles, then, can help us overcome the false dichotomy between truth and love.

Setting the Stage

In 2 and 3 John, John writes to the church again, probably in Asia Minor. While 2 John is addressed to a particular church, addressing the entire community as the "elect lady," 3 John is addressed to an individual in the church named Gaius. One can see very much the same conflict going on in 2 and 3 John that was addressed at length in 1 John. There are people in the church who refuse to love and who refuse to confess the truth that Jesus Christ came in the flesh.

113. In what areas do you sense a possible conflict between truth and love?

114. How do you resolve this conflict?

2 John

John's greeting at the beginning of the Letter ends with the phrase "in truth and love" (2 John 3). These words, *truth* and *love*, introduce the two major themes of 2 John. The first half of the Letter deals with God's command to love, while the second half deals with the necessity to confess the truth that Jesus Christ came in the flesh.

115. Read 2 John 1–6. As he does in 1 John, so here John reminds his readers that the commandment to love is not new; they have had it from the beginning. He does not, however, give precise information about how the original recipients of his Letter were falling short of this command. From what you remember of 1 John, sketch how John's readers were failing to love. You may wish to review the following passages:

a. 1 John 2:15–17

b. 1 John 3:16–18

c. 1 John 4:19–21

116. Read 2 John 7–13. John states that the deceivers refuse to confess "the coming of Jesus Christ in the flesh" (v. 7). Why do you think John singles out this doctrine as key? You may wish to review your discussion in Lesson 1.

117. John says that the consequence of this erroneous belief is that such a person "does not have God" (v. 9). John does not explicitly

discuss love at this point, but why do you think it would be difficult to love without faith in the incarnation?

3 John

This short Letter deals with support and opposition within the congregation to which John is writing. The Letter is addressed to an individual named Gaius, who welcomed a group of Christian missionaries. John cites this as evidence of Gaius's love (v. 6). On the other hand, a man named Diotrephes refused to welcome the brothers.

118. Read 3 John 1–8. There is precedent in the New Testament for missionaries sometimes to depend on people of goodwill for their physical needs. Where do missionaries get their support according to the following passages?

a. Matthew 10:5–15

b. 2 Corinthians 12:14–18

c. 1 Thessalonians 2:9

119. Given the example of Paul in the last two passages, it may be that traveling missionaries did not always feel comfortable asking for support. How does offering such support, even when it is not asked for, benefit not only the recipient but the giver as well?

120. Read 3 John 9–15. Diotrephes is the opposite of Gaius because he refuses to welcome the brothers. But his problem is not only with love. How does John imply that Diotrephes has a problem with the truth as well?

God's Word for Today

Since truth and love are the two major themes of these two Letters, we want to think about how truth and love function in our life in the Church today. Truth and love are not opposed to each other, but are in fact inseparable from each other. No one can keep one without the other.

121. To what concrete acts of love do you think the truths of Christianity should lead?

122. How would you respond to someone who claims that the Church should focus on acts of love and not worry so much about the truth?

In Closing

Close with prayer. Sing or read the words of "Spread the Reign of God the Lord" (*LSB* 830, stanzas 1–4).

Spread the reign of God the Lord,
Spoken, written, mighty Word;
Ev'rywhere His creatures call
To His heav'nly banquet hall.

Tell how God the Father's will
Made the world, upholds it still,
How His own dear Son He gave
Us from sin and death to save.

Tell of our Redeemer's grace,
Who, to save our human race
And to pay rebellion's price,
Gave Himself as sacrifice.

Tell of God the Spirit giv'n
Now to guide us on to heav'n,
Strong and holy, just and true,
Working both to will and do.

Leader Notes

These notes are provided as a "safety net," a place to turn for help in answering questions and for enriching discussion. They will not answer every question raised in your class. Please read them, along with the questions, before class. Consult them in class only after exploring the Bible references and discussing what they teach. Please note the different abilities of your class members. Some will easily find the Bible passages listed in this study; others will struggle. To make participation easier, team up members of the class. For example, if a question asks you to look up several passages, assign one passage to one group, the second to another, and so on. Divide the work! Let participants present the answers they discover.

Preparing to Teach 1, 2, and 3 John

To prepare to lead this study, read through the Books of 1, 2, and 3 John. You might review the introduction to these books in the *Concordia Self-Study Bible* or a Bible handbook. A map of the Roman world (especially the lands surrounding the Mediterranean Sea) will show you where Asia Minor is, where the recipients of the Letters probably lived.

The materials in these notes are designed to help you in leading others through this portion of the Holy Scriptures. Nevertheless, this booklet is to be an aid to—and not a substitute for—your own study of and preparation for teaching the Books of 1, 2, and 3 John.

If you have the opportunity, you will find it helpful to make use of other biblical reference works in the course of your study. For example, you may find it helpful to refer to Mark A. Jeske, *The General Epistles*, People's Bible Commentary (St. Louis: Concordia Publishing House, 2004). This book has a section on John's Epistles.

Group Bible Study

Group Bible study means mutual learning from one another under the guidance of a leader. The Bible is an inexhaustible resource. No one person can discover all it has to offer. In any class, many eyes see many things, things that can be applied to many life situations. The leader should resist the temptation to give the answers and so act as an authority. This teaching approach stifles participation by individual members and can actually hamper learning. As a general rule, don't give interpretation. Instead, develop interpreters. In other words, don't explain what the learners can discover by themselves. This is not to say that the leader shouldn't share insights and information gained by his or her class members during the lesson, engage them in meaningful sharing and discussion, or lead them to a summary of the lesson at the close.

Have a chalkboard and chalk or newsprint and marker available to emphasize significant points of the lesson. Rephrase your inquiries or the inquiries of participants as questions, problems, or issues. This provokes thought. Keep discussion to the point. List the answers given on the chalkboard or newsprint. Then determine the most vital points made in the discussion. Ask additional questions to fill gaps.

The aim of every Bible study is to help people grow spiritually, not merely in biblical and theological knowledge, but in Christian thinking and living. This means growth in Christian attitudes, insights, and skills for Christian living. The focus of this course must be the Church and the world of our day. The guiding question will be this: What does the Lord teach us for life today through 1, 2, and 3 John?

Teaching the New Testament

Teaching a New Testament Letter that was originally written for and read to first-century Christians can become merely ancient history if not applied to life in our times. Leaders need to understand the time and culture in which the Letter was written. They need to understand the historical situation of the Early Church and the social and cultural setting in which that Church existed. Such background information can clarify the original purpose and meaning of the Letter and shed light on its meaning for Christians today. For this reason, Bible commentaries and other reference works are indispensable when it comes to leading Bible studies.

Teaching the Bible can easily degenerate into mere moralizing, in which do-goodism or rules become substitutes for the Gospel, and sanctification is confused with justification. Actually, justified sinners are moved to a totally new life not by Law but by God's grace. Their faith is always at work for Christ in every context of life. Meaningful, personal Christianity consists of a loving trust in God that is evidenced in love for others. Having experienced God's free grace and forgiveness, Christians daily work in their world to reflect the will of God for people in every area of human endeavor.

Christian leaders are Gospel-oriented, not Law-oriented; they distinguish between the two. Both Law and Gospel are necessary. The Gospel will mean nothing unless we first have been crushed by the Law and see our sinfulness. There is no genuine Christianity if faith is not followed by lives pleasing to God. In fact, genuine faith is inseparable from life. The Gospel alone gives us the new heart that causes us to love God and our neighbor.

Pace Your Teaching

The lessons in this course of study are designed for a study session of at least an hour in length. If it is the desire and intent of the class to complete an entire lesson each session, it will be necessary for you to summarize the content of certain answers or biblical references in order to preserve time. Asking various class members to look up different Bible passages and to read them aloud to the rest of the class will save time over having every class member look up each reference.

Also, you may not want to cover every question in each lesson. This may lead to undue haste and frustration. Be selective. Pace your teaching. Spend no more than five to ten minutes opening the lesson. During the lesson, get the sweep of meaning. Occasionally stop to help the class gain understanding of a word or concept. Allow approximately five minutes for closing and announcements.

Should your group have more than a one-hour class period, you can take it more leisurely, but do not allow any lesson to drag and become tiresome. Keep it moving. Keep it alive. Keep it meaningful. Eliminate some questions, and restrict yourself to those questions most meaningful to the members of the class. If most members study the text at home, they can report their findings, and the time gained can be applied to relating the lesson to life.

Good Preparation

Good preparation by the leader usually affects the pleasure and satisfaction the class will experience.

Suggestions to the Leader for Using the Study Guide

This set of lessons is designed to aid Bible study, that is, to aid a consideration of the written Word of God, with discussion and personal application growing out of the text at hand.

The typical lesson is divided into these sections:

1. Theme Verse
2. Objectives
3. Questions and Answers
4. Closing

The theme verse and objectives give you, the leader, assistance in arousing the interest of the group in the concepts of the lesson. Focus on stimulating minds. Do not linger too long over the introductory remarks.

The questions and answers provide the real spadework necessary for Bible study. Here the class digs, uncovers, and discovers; it gets the facts and observes them. Comments from the leader are needed only to the extent that they help the group understand the text. The questions in this guide, corresponding to sections within the text, are intended to help the participants discover the meaning of the text.

Having determined what the text says, the class is ready to apply the message. Having heard, read, marked, and learned the Word of God, they can proceed to digest it inwardly through discussion, evaluation, and application. This is done, as this guide suggests, by taking the truths found in Scripture and applying them to the world and Christianity in general and then to one's personal Christian life. Class time may not permit discussion of all questions and topics. In preparation, you may need to select one or two and focus on them. Close the session by reviewing one important truth from the lesson.

Remember, the Word of God is sacred, but this study guide is not. The notes in this section offer only guidelines and suggestions. Do not hesitate to alter the guidelines or substitute others to meet your needs and the needs of the participants. Adapt your teaching plan to your class and your class period.

Good teaching directs the learner to discover for himself or herself. For the teacher, this means directing the learner but not giving the learner answers. Directing understanding takes preparation. Choose the verses that should be looked up in Scripture ahead of time. What discussion questions will you ask and at what points will you ask them? Write them in the margin of your study guide. Involve class members, but give them clear directions. What practical actions might you propose for the week following the lesson? Which of the items do you consider most important for your class?

Consider how you can best use your teaching period. Do you have forty-five minutes, an hour, or an hour and a half? If time is short, what should you cut? Learn to become a wise steward of class time.

Plan a brief opening devotion using members of the class. At the end, be sure to take time to summarize the lesson or have a class member do it.

Remember to pray frequently for yourself and your class. May God the Holy Spirit bless your study and your leading of others into the comforting truths of God's Christ-centered Word.

Lesson 1

The Word of Life

Theme verse: *The life was made manifest, and we have seen it, and testify to it and proclaim to you the eternal life, which was with the Father and was made manifest to us.*

1 John 1:2

Objectives

By the power of the Holy Spirit working through God's Word, we will

- reflect on the importance of Christ's incarnation;
- identify the teaching of John's opponents;
- grow in our fellowship with Christ and with one another.

Setting the Stage

1. Eyewitness testimony is an important way to establish facts in a court of law.

2. Answers may vary. Since refutation of error can seem confrontational, some people may be uncomfortable with it. However, since the truth of the faith is critical to our life in Christ, others may welcome it.

We Have Touched the Word of Life

3. John the Baptist pointed Jesus out by saying, "Behold, the Lamb of God, who takes away the sin of the world!" (John 1:29). Jesus washed the disciples' feet (John 13:1–11). Thomas put his hand in Jesus' side (John 20:27). John leaned on Jesus' breast at the Last Supper (John 21:20, see especially the KJV).

4. By becoming flesh, the Word shows the value of the physical creation, and indeed he saves the physical creation. If creation were not valuable,

a. the world and our bodies would be curses, not gifts, from God;

b. Jesus would only have *appeared* to die because someone who has no body cannot die a physical death;

c. the Lord would certainly not give us His body and blood to eat and drink because He would have no body and blood;

d. there would be no resurrection if our bodies had no value.

John's Opponents

5. a. 1 John 1:8: they thought they had no sin.

b. 1 John 2:4: they felt no need to keep God's Commandments.

c. 1 John 2:22: they denied that Jesus is the Christ.

d. 1 John 4:2–3: they deny that Jesus came in the flesh.

6. Answers may vary. A secular worldview may lead people to a similar indifference about what they do with their bodies.

Fellowship

7. The Lord's Supper brings us into fellowship with Christ in His body and blood and with one another.

8. Answers may vary. Fellowship means we are not alone, but we are part of a family. Membership in Christ's family brings with it not only companionship but also forgiveness of sins and eternal life.

God's Word for Today

9. When we rely on the eyewitness testimony of others, we have to believe what we ourselves did not see. Also, it is possible for eyewitness testimony to err. John assures us that his testimony does not err by stressing that he saw and touched Jesus.

10. Answers may vary. The Word and Sacraments give us a concrete and tangible promise that God has accepted us. When we know how we stand with God, we are then able to tell others.

Lesson 2

Light and Darkness

Theme verse: *If we confess our sins, He is faithful and just to forgive us our sins and to cleanse us from all unrighteousness.*

1 John 1:9

Objectives

By the power of the Holy Spirit working through God's Word, we will
- identify the central message of the Scriptures;
- learn how to describe sin in the Christian life more precisely;
- experience the manifold ways God forgives sin.

Setting the Stage

11. Answers may vary. Not all participants may feel comfortable answering. Feelings that accompany sin may be diverse, such as guilt, numbness, or even a thrill.

12. The "right answer" is through God's Word and Sacrament, but more important at this point is to let the participants describe what they rely on in practice. The role of Word and Sacrament will come out in the rest of the lesson.

God Is Light

13. To say that God is light means that He is holy and that sin is utterly foreign to Him. This could be terrifying since it means that He does not tolerate sin, but it is also comforting if we understand that through Christ, our sin is paid for and we can, with confidence, stand before God in His holiness.

14. Luke summarizes the Christian message in terms of repentance and forgiveness. When John says that "God is light," he implies the necessity of both repentance and forgiveness since God does not tolerate sin. So both Luke and John identify the central Christian message in a way that recognizes that sin must be dealt with.

Walking in the Light

15. b. Someone who sins but confesses it. The answer cannot be a, since there is no one who does not sin. Neither can the answer be c, because John says those who deny their sin deceive themselves.

16. If we do not confess our sins, we deceive ourselves.

a. If we do not confess, we make God out to be a liar.

b. This is tantamount to saying God is the devil, since the devil is the father of lies (John 8:44).

17. Answers may vary. The point here is to let the participants voice their anxieties.

18. Again, answers may vary. You may wish to point out the comfort that comes with the forgiveness of sins that, in the end, outweighs whatever anxieties we may have about confessing. You may also point out that sometimes, you have to set aside time to do something that is important to you.

19. The absolution says, "As a called and ordained servant of Christ, and by His authority, I therefore forgive you all your sins" (*LSB*, p. 151).

a. Even the Pharisees recognized that only God can forgive sins (Mark 2:7).

b. The pastor is speaking not on his own authority, but on the authority of Christ, who through His Church delegates this to His called and ordained servants (John 20:21–23).

c. We have no doubt that our sins are forgiven because Christ has promised that the absolution spoken by the pastor is valid also in heaven.

God's Word for Today

20. Whenever Christians are tempted to minimize or excuse their sins rather than confess them, they are tempted to walk in darkness.

21. Answers may vary. One possible answer is that to "walk in the light" is not so much about being holy as it is about confessing sins and receiving God's rich forgiveness through Christ.

Lesson 3

Love and Hate

Theme verse: *Whoever says he is in the light and hates his brother is still in darkness. Whoever loves his brother abides in the light, and in him there is no cause for stumbling.*

1 John 2:9–10

Objectives

By the power of the Holy Spirit working through God's Word, we will

- understand more fully the saving work of Christ as propitiation;
- learn how to address hate;
- learn how love is a consistent theme throughout the Scriptures, but also how Christ makes it new.

Setting the Stage

22. Answers may vary. Some people try to know God by examining their own hearts, assuming that He reveals Himself there. Others try to use reason to deduce truths about God from nature or from philosophy. Still others think they can approach God through moral striving.

23. Some do, and some don't. Especially the secular mind-set assumes that people should decide for themselves what is good for them; they need not consult an authority for this.

Jesus, the Propitiation for Our Sins

24. Participants should articulate that Jesus places His own blood and righteousness before the Father to plead for our pardon and acceptance.

25. It depends on how we view sin. If we see sin as something we shouldn't do, but we want to do it anyway, then it is possible to misunderstand the message of forgiveness as a license to sin all the more (see Romans 6:15). However, if we have the correct understanding of sin as something that enslaves us in darkness and death, we will rejoice to be rid of it when we hear the message of propitiation.

Lying and Telling the Truth

26. John says we know this if we keep God's Commandments. However, participants may not always be comforted by this because this criterion can often result in mixed messages.

27. These passages clarify that John knows that his readers sin. Therefore, John should not be understood to suggest that a sinless life is what gives us confidence that we know God.

28. Most likely, when John writes about the love of God being perfected in us, he means that God's love for us reaches its goal when it moves us to love our neighbor. Thus God keeps His Word.

Love: A Command Both Old and New

29. Leviticus 19:18 shows that "you shall love your neighbor as yourself" is a command present already in the Old Testament.

30. The new element that Jesus adds on Maundy Thursday is that we are to love one another "just as I have loved you." So Jesus' love becomes the perfect model of what our love should look like.

31. Jesus' love is totally concerned with the good of others. He is willing to die for people who do not deserve it.

Hate: A Life in Darkness

32. Answers may vary since the participants are drawing on their own experience.

33. John says that the Christian's response to hate should be love. This is because God has first responded to our hate and the hate of others with His own love in Christ. Once we appreciate how we did not

deserve the good things we received from God, it becomes possible to give others good things that they do not deserve.

Do Not Love the World

34. John is referring to people, angels, and anything else that is opposed to God.

35. John is not saying that the physical creation is evil. God created it good, and John stresses how the Word of life came in a physical way (1 John 1:1; 4:2; John 1:14).

God's Word for Today

36. Most likely, participants will recognize that they do keep the Commandments in some way, but not perfectly. It is also possible to say that, in the eyes of God and through faith, we do keep the Commandments perfectly because Christ has paid for our sins and kept the Law in our place.

37. John teaches that we can have confidence that we know the Father when we see ourselves keeping the Commandments. Our ultimate confidence, however, comes from what God promises in His Word and Sacraments.

Lesson 4

Christ and Antichrists

Theme verse: *No one who denies the Son has the Father. Whoever confesses the Son has the Father also.*

1 John 2:23

Objectives

By the power of the Holy Spirit working through God's Word, we will

- define *antichrist* in the various ways the Scriptures use the term;
- learn how the Holy Spirit operates through His "anointing";
- construct a way of discerning the truth of claims that are purportedly from the Holy Spirit.

Setting the Stage

38. Answers will vary. Probably participants will think of one figure of ultimate evil.

39. Answers will vary.

The Coming of the Antichrists(s)

40. Antichrists come from within the Church but do not remain with the Church (1 John 2:19). They deny that Jesus is the Christ (2:22). They were apparently claiming some new truth that was different than what John's readers had heard from the beginning (2:24).

41. John's description focuses on what the antichrists say about Christ. The antichrists are not political figures who usher in worldwide destruction; they are false teachers from within the Church.

The Anointing

42. John is obviously teaching his readers as a father teaches his children. His point is that they do not need the teaching of the false teachers.

43. In light of the fact that John himself teaches his readers, as well as the fact that there was actually an office of "teacher" in the Early Church (see Ephesians 4:11), John does not mean to say there should be no teachers in the Church.

44. We need teachers to teach us God's Word.

45. We do not need teachers, however, to teach us some new message beyond or in contradiction to God's Word. This is what John's opponents were doing. So when John tells his readers they need no one to teach them, he is thinking particularly of this kind of teaching that goes beyond God's Word.

God's Word for Today

46. Any false teachers could be classified as antichrists in John's sense of the term. The Lutheran Confessions also identify the pope as the Antichrist because that office denies the Gospel of justification by faith alone and has claimed that everyone must be subject to the pope in order to be saved. (This claim was made in the papal bull *Unam sanctam* in 1302. See Smalcald Articles II IV (The Papacy) in the Book of Concord, *Concordia*, pp. 268–70.) However, this use of "antichrist" corresponds more to Paul's discussion of a single antichrist figure in 2 Thessalonians 2:1–12 than to John's discussion of multiple antichrists.

47. John tells us not to look for new revelations of the Spirit beyond the Word that we have heard from the beginning, recorded in Holy Scriptures. Therefore, the Scriptures remain the ultimate authority for any claim about what God says or does.

Lesson 5

Children of God; Children of the Devil

Theme verse: *See what kind of love the Father has given us, that we should be called children of God; and so we are.*

1 John 3:1

Objectives

By the power of the Holy Spirit working through God's Word, we will

- come to a greater appreciation of God's love for us;
- understand the implications of God's demand for perfection;
- come to a point where we can look forward to Judgment Day with confidence.

Setting the Stage

48. It can be attractive because it makes us look good if we can claim to live without sin.

49. We should react to God's demand for perfection in two ways: repent of falling short of it and receive forgiveness; make every effort to live according to God's commands.

The Father's Love for Us

50. God has given us His love by making us His children. Our love for others, in turn, marks us as God's children. The world does not know God. Therefore, it also does not know us.

51. Answers may vary.

52. On that day, we will see Christ as He is, and we will be made like Him.

53. We will become imperishable and immortal, and death will be destroyed.

54. When we think of our sins, we may feel shame. But when we think of the salvation Christ accomplished for us on the cross, we can feel confident.

55. John says that hope in Christ's salvation on the day of His return makes us pure. This is very similar to saying that we are saved by faith.

The End of Sin

56. No. "If we say we have not sinned, we make Him a liar, and His word is not in us" (1 John 1:10).

57. "Everyone who makes a practice of sinning" are those whose life is characterized primarily by sin. They sin and do not care that they do. It defines their life. No one can be like this and still be a Christian.

58. John certainly says that a Christian has sin (1 John 1:8), but a Christian does not make a practice of sinning, that is, a Christian does not allow sin to define his or her life, but rather seeks God's forgiveness.

God's Word for Today

59. Participants may refer to good works that they do, since John says these things are evidence of being God's children (1 John 2:29). They may also refer to God's promises to them in Word and Sacrament.

60. Since Christians do have sin (1 John 1:8, 10), there will always be contrary evidence when we look at our lives. Therefore, we can find our most solid basis of assurance in God's promises in Word and Sacrament.

Lesson 6

Love and Murder

Theme verse: *For this is the message that you have heard from the beginning, that we should love one another.*

1 John 3:11

Objectives

By the power of the Holy Spirit working through God's Word, we will
- learn how the story of Cain and Abel teaches us how to love;
- learn how Jesus' death on the cross teaches us how to love;
- find confidence before God.

Setting the Stage

61. Answers may vary. One common popular definition to note is that love is a feeling. In this lesson, we will learn that love is more than a feeling.

62. Answers may vary.

The Example of Cain

63. Cain was jealous because God accepted Abel's sacrifice, but not his. God did not accept Cain's sacrifice because Cain did not "do well" (Genesis 4:7), that is, he did not offer his sacrifice in faith as Abel had (Hebrews 11:4).

64. John says Cain killed Abel because Cain's deeds were evil and Abel's were righteous.

65. Genesis 4:7 does note that Cain did not "do well." This implies his sacrifice was rejected because of his evil deeds. Both

Genesis and John point to Cain's jealousy and anger over not being accepted by God as motivations for murder.

What Love Looks Like

66. Laying down our lives is the ultimate form of self-sacrificial love. But any act in which we put the needs of others ahead of our own needs is related to this kind of love.

67. As Jesus makes clear, in God's eyes hatred is tantamount to murder.

68. For John, real love is not a feeling but an action. Therefore, it makes no sense to talk about a feeling of love or a claim of love that is not backed up by action (see 1 John 3:18).

The Confidence That Love Gives

69. Love can reassure our hearts. Since it comes from God, it is evidence that God is at work in our lives. However, in this life love is not the clearest evidence because Christians still have sin.

70. To Christians who are not reassured by the love they see in their own hearts, John offers them the comfort that God is "greater than our heart" (1 John 3:20).

71. Confess your sins, and receive God's forgiveness for the sake of Christ.

God's Word for Today

72. Answers may vary.
73. Answers may vary.

Lesson 7

Spirit of God; Spirit of the Antichrist

Theme verse: *Beloved, do not believe every spirit, but test the spirits to see whether they are from God.*

1 John 4:1

Objectives

By the power of the Holy Spirit working through God's Word, we will

- learn how to test claims about what God is saying;
- apply this knowledge to an actual claim about a new message from the Holy Spirit;
- learn to see the combat between God and the world.

Setting the Stage

74. Answers may vary. Some churches, such as Pentecostal churches, claim direct revelations from the Spirit. Others, such as Evangelical churches, claim a more vague "leading" by the Spirit.

75. The point is not to arrive at the "right answer" right away (which is to evaluate all claims by the Scriptures), but to get various viewpoints on the table.

Testing the Spirits

76. a. Deuteronomy 18:20–22: True prophecy must be spoken in the Lord's name, and it must come true.

b. Deuteronomy 13:1–3: Prophecy is to be judged by its content. Prophecy that urges people to go after other gods cannot be true.

c. Matthew 16:13–23: Here again the issue is content. Jesus says that Peter's answer, "You are the Christ, the Son of the living God," was revealed to Peter by God. However, when Peter tries to prevent Jesus from going through with His suffering and death, Jesus identifies him as Satan.

d. Galatians 1:8: No message that contradicts the Gospel can be true, no matter who delivers it.

e. 1 Corinthians 12:3: The spirit can be identified by what is being said about Jesus.

77. Aside from being made in the Lord's name and coming true (if it is a prediction), we should judge all teaching on the basis of the Scriptures, especially what the Scriptures say about Christ.

78. Answers may vary. Some deny that Jesus came in the flesh, so they think of Him only as a spirit being, as did the Gnostics. Others consider Him a mere human being and thus deny His divinity, as does Islam.

Overcoming the World

79. Answers may vary. John's description puts the mundane routines of our lives into the context of a cosmic battle. Humble acts of caring for our neighbor as well as witnessing to the Gospel are by no means insignificant; they are all part of God's battle against Satan. We have comfort in that we know that God has already won the battle for us in Christ, and He allows us to share in that victory.

80. Even among Christians, messages of health and wealth sometimes gain a following, despite the fact that the self-serving attitude such messages foster is at odds with Jesus' attitude of self-sacrifice.

God's Word for Today

81. The sermon takes something that the Scriptures identify as a sin and in essence blames it on God by labeling it a God-given identity. This is an example of dealing with sin not by confessing it, but by denying that it is a sin. See 1 John 1:8–10.

82. God demonstrated His love for us not by tolerating sin, but by sending His Son as the propitiation for our sin so that it may be

forgiven. Likewise, we show our love for God not by denying what Scripture calls a sin, but by affirming and keeping God's Commandments (1 John 3:24). This does not mean that the Church should attempt to persecute homosexuals, but the Church should address this sin like it would address any other: through the proper distinction of Law and Gospel (1 John 1:5–10).

Lesson 8

Love and Fear

Theme verse: *We love because He first loved us.*

1 John 4:19

Objectives

By the power of the Holy Spirit working through God's Word, we will

- learn how God defines love;
- identify the sources of fear in our lives;
- grow in confidence that God's love in Christ overcomes our fear.

Setting the Stage

83. Answers may vary.
84. Answers may vary.

God's Love for Us

85. First, God's love is something that can be seen. John says it is "made manifest." Second, God's love involved sacrificing His only Son by sending Him into the world to die on the cross. In John, the "world" is an evil place where the devil holds sway. Third, God's love gives life. Ordinary human love can also be seen, and in some cases it can be intensely self-sacrificing (see Romans 5:7). However, ordinary human love can never give life.

86. Our worth in God's eyes cannot be estimated on the basis of our love for Him. Rather, it is estimated on the basis of His love for us. That means that other people have this same worth.

87. John 1:18 says that the Son has made the Father known, and 1 John 4:11–12 says that God is made known through our love. Both are true, but the John 1:18 passage is primary. God's love in Christ comes first, and then our love.

Perfect Love Casts Out Fear

88. Answers may vary. Since we are not yet what we will be (1 John 3:2), we still find sin permeating our lives. For some, this may be a source of fear.

89. If we are secure in God's love for us, which He gives before and apart from our love for Him, then we can also view our own love as evidence of God's work in our lives. However, if we imagine that we gain God's favor by loving Him, then the imperfection of our love will always provoke doubt. God's love for us in Christ is our security and our comfort.

90. When John speaks of perfect love, he probably has in mind the perfection of love that we will possess when Christ returns. In heaven, there will be no fear or preaching about punishment. On the other hand, the Small Catechism addresses our lives here and now. Since we are both saint and sinner in this life, our works still have a dual motivation of fear and love. However, we can live in certainty that love has the final word.

God's Word for Today

91. Someone motivated by fear would say she has done her duty by going to church. She might fear that bad things will happen to her during the week if she skips a service. On the other hand, a person motivated by love goes to church gladly to hear and learn God's Word and receive His blessings in His Word and Sacraments. These blessings both inspire and enable praise.

92. A person motivated by fear may assume that honesty makes one good in God's eyes. Or, he or she may recognize that the consequences of dishonesty would be unpleasant. However, someone motivated by love practices honesty because God first gave him or her respect and love; in response, that person wants to behave in the same way toward others. Fear and love are both legitimate motivations, because they are responses to God's Law and Gospel, respectively, but John wants to move the Christian to operate out of love.

Lesson 9

Faith

Theme verse: *And this is the victory that has overcome
the world—our faith.*

1 John 5:4

Objectives

By the power of the Holy Spirit working through God's Word,
we will
- explore how faith in Christ is a victory;
- relate faith to God's Law and to the world;
- learn how the Spirit, the water, and the blood testify about
  Christ.

Setting the Stage

93. The title "Christ" means that Jesus has received an anointing
by the Holy Spirit from the Father. This anointing sent Him on His
mission to save the world. To believe that Jesus is the Christ, then, is to
trust in the salvation He won for us through His life, death, and
resurrection.

94. Jesus' Baptism is perhaps the most important event that
designated Him as the Christ because He was anointed with the Holy
Spirit (Matthew 3:16).

Faith and Works

95. Answers may vary. Most likely, participants will resonate
with Paul's description in Romans 7, in which he expresses the
difficulty of keeping God's Law.

96. When we receive rest from Jesus, the forgiveness of sins, then the "yoke" of His commands are not burdensome because the threat of punishment has been overcome.

97. Faith overcomes the world because everyone who believes that Jesus is the Christ has been born of God (1 John 5:1). Since God has overcome the world through Christ's death and resurrection, we His children share in that victory.

The Spirit, the Water, and the Blood

98. a. John 1:29–34: Jesus is baptized in water, and the Spirit descends on Him, identifying Him as the Son of God.

b. John 2:1–11: Jesus turns water into wine; this is the first sign (miracle) that showed Jesus' glory.

c. John 19:34–35: Blood and water flowed from Jesus' side. John emphasizes this fact but does not interpret it in this passage.

99. None of the passages has all three (Spirit, water, and blood). Jesus receives His anointing (became the "Christ") at His Baptism, the water turned into wine shows His deity, and the blood and water flowing from His side highlights the importance of His death in God's plan of salvation.

100. a. John 20:21–23: Christ gives the Holy Spirit to forgive sins in the absolution.

b. John 3:5: Christ uses water to give new birth.

c. John 6:53–55: Christ's flesh and blood give us life.

God's Word for Today

101. Answers may vary. One possible answer is that because faith in Christ is victory over the world, we might experience less anxiety.

102. Answers may vary. Participants may mention things like saying grace or having devotions, or they may focus on thought processes or what is important throughout the day.

Lesson 10

Prayer

Theme verse: *And this is the confidence that we have toward Him, that if we ask anything according to His will He hears us.*

1 John 5:14

Objectives

By the power of the Holy Spirit working through God's Word, we will

- learn what Christ promises about prayer;
- distinguish the sin that leads to death from sin that does not lead to death;
- review the basic message of 1 John.

Setting the Stage

103. Answers may vary.

104. Answers may vary, but common answers might be busyness, uncertainty about what to pray for, or even boredom. Ultimately, our failure to pray or laxity in prayer is a faith issue.

Christ's Promise concerning Prayer

105. 1 John 5:14–15: God will grant us anything we ask according to His will.

a. John 14:13–14: Jesus will grant anything we ask in His name.

b. Matthew 7:7: If you ask, you will be answered.

106. When we pray according to God's will, we pray with the understanding that He knows better than we what is best for us. Therefore, we trust His judgment more than our own. That is why the

three men in Daniel 3:16–18 could cheerfully contemplate the possibility that God might not deliver them from the fire. They knew that if God chose to act in this way, it would be the best thing for them.

Sin That Leads to Death

107. If we say we have no sin, we deceive ourselves and make God out to be a liar. This is tantamount to making God the devil because the devil is the father of lies. Similarly, the Pharisees said that the Spirit by which Jesus cast out demons was the devil. In both instances, God was made out to be the devil.

108. John does not give specifics, but we can say that sin that does not lead to death is sin that is forgiven. Sin that leads to death is sin that is obstinately denied, for which forgiveness is neither sought nor received. It would make no sense to ask God to forgive that kind of sin; the person does not want forgiveness. It would still be possible, however, to pray for the conversion of such a person.

Conclusion

109. The contrast between the devil (or the world) and God picks up all the dualities we have looked at in this study: light and dark, truth and lies, love and murder, and so forth.

110. Answers may vary. One prominent feature in 1 John is the cosmic battle raging between God and the world. God has overcome the world, which will ultimately come to light on the Day of Judgment.

God's Word for Today

111. Answers may vary.

112. Hopefully, the promises Christ makes about prayer in the Bible will encourage the participants to go to Him more often in prayer.

Lesson 11

2 and 3 John

Theme verse: *Grace, mercy, and peace will be with us, from God the Father and from Jesus Christ the Father's Son, in truth and love.*

2 John 3

Objectives

By the power of the Holy Spirit working through God's Word, we will
- consider how we may be tempted to see love and truth as incompatible;
- learn how John says they go together;
- gain a more concrete picture of love.

Setting the Stage

113. Answers may vary.

114. Answers may vary. The two extremes would be either to say that only love matters, so truth claims make no difference, or to say that being right is all that counts, so it does not matter how we treat people.

2 John

115. a. 1 John 2:15–17: John warns his readers against loving the world.

b. 1 John 3:16–18: John warns his readers against failing to meet a brother's needs.

c. 1 John 4:19–21: John warns his readers against hating a brother.

116. Gnosticism, a later heresy that had similar teachings to those of John's opponents, taught that the material world was evil. Anyone with this mind-set would never want to say that Jesus Christ came in the flesh, because that would sound like He became evil.

117. In the incarnation, Christ came down from His throne in heaven and took on human flesh to give His life for our salvation. This is the love of God that causes our love. As John says in his First Epistle, "We love because He first loved us" (1 John 4:19).

3 John

118. a. Matthew 10:5–15: The disciples were to stay with people in whatever town they go to and receive support from them.

b. 2 Corinthians 12:14–18: Paul did not accept help from those to whom he was writing.

c. 1 Thessalonians 2:9: Paul and his companions worked to support themselves even while serving as missionaries.

119. Supporting such people obviously helps them in their mission, and John tells us that it makes us fellow workers with them.

120. John says Diotrephes "does not acknowledge our authority" (3 John 9). This implies that he did not accept the message that John preached.

God's Word for Today

121. Answers may vary. When John gives concrete examples, he focuses on caring for the needy brother (1 John 3:17; 3 John 8).

122. This is a false dichotomy. The truth of what Christ has done for our salvation is what enables us to love. "We love because He first loved us" (1 John 4:19). Therefore, any talk of love without truth is empty.